The Penny Bank

by John Tomlinson
illustrated by Julie Downing

HOUGHTON MIFFLIN   BOSTON

Printed in China

ISBN 10: 0-618-89963-4
ISBN 13: 978-0-618-89963-0

9 10 11 12 13 0940 20 19 18 17 16 15
4500534882

For Madison's birthday, her grandfather gave her a special present—a penny bank. The bank looked like a basketball player, and if you put a penny in her hand and pushed her foot down, she shot the penny into a basket!

"Just make sure you keep taking shots," Madison's grandfather said. "You know what they say: a penny saved is a penny earned!"

Madison and her little brother Michael were trying to save as many pennies as they could.

They liked putting coins into the bank, but they liked taking them out, too. Last week there were 88 pennies in the bank, but then they took 40 out to buy themselves a treat.

Read·Think·Write How many pennies were left in the bank?

They got better at saving. One Saturday, Michael brought Madison 2 dimes.

"They won't work in the bank," he complained.

"Well, we can fix that," Madison said. "A dime is worth ten pennies, so let's ask Dad to trade with us."

Dad was more than happy to get rid of pennies! They were heavy!

Read·Think·Write How many pennies should Madison and Michael's father give them?

Michael began putting the pennies into the bank, and Madison continued her homework. The next problem was $20 - 11$. She couldn't subtract 1 from zero, but she could do something else. "It's just like trading a dime for pennies!" she thought.

The 20 was like 2 dimes, or twenty cents. She could trade 1 dime for ten pennies.

Then, the numbers would be grouped to subtract.

Read·Think·Write How many ones are in the answer? How many tens?

As Madison finished the problem, Michael said, "It's full!" They emptied the bank and counted the pennies: there were 212 in all.

"We really did a good job saving," Madison said. "I think we deserve a treat."

They stuffed their pockets with pennies and walked to the corner store.

Read·Think·Write If two cookies cost 88 cents, how much money do Madison and Michael have left?

At school on Monday, Madison's teacher said she had done a great job on her math work. Her teacher said she really seemed to understand regrouping now. Madison told him about the penny bank.

"Well," said Madison's teacher, "you know what they say: a penny saved is a lesson learned!"

1. Subtract.

26
− 5

   Did you need to regroup? Explain.

2. Subtract.

42
− 9

   Did you need to regroup? Explain.

3. Show how you regrouped in Question 2.

Activity

   Visualize Take some play pennies, nickels, dimes, and quarters. Make two piles with the coins, and write down the number in each pile. Subtract the smaller number from the larger number.